Subterranean Light

Subterranean Light

Poems by

Susanne West

Los Altos, CA
www.HyenaPress.com

Copyright © 2021 by My Hyena Group

All rights reserved. No part of this book may be reproduced or transmitted in any form or by any means, electronic or mechanical, including photocopying, recording, or by an information storage and retrieval system—except by a reviewer who may quote brief passages in a review to be printed in a magazine, newspaper, or on the Web—without permission in writing from the copyright owner.

This book is published by Enlightened Hyena Press.
2310 Homestead Rd, C1 #125
Los Altos, CA
www.HyenaPress.com

First Paperback Edition
ISBN 978-0-9842239-5-4

Cover Design & Book Design: EH Designs

ATTENTION ORGANIZATIONS—DISCOUNT ON BULK PURCHASES AVAILABLE.

For information, please contact the publisher:
www.HyenaPress.com, info@hyenapress.com, (408) 819-3715

For my family, with love and gratitude.

Contents

Ordinary Grace

    Faces 13

    Tell the Stories 14

    Every Life 16

    How We Are Helped 17

    Nourishing the Poet 19

    Mystic Jammies 20

    Butterfly Medicine 21

    Sarah Kisses 23

    The Shape of Comfort 25

    This Bed Will Never End................................ 26

    Fading Light... 27

    How to Find Poems...28

What Illness Reveals

    Being Will Have Its Way 33

    The Last Chemo 35

    You Are Broken and You Are Whole............38

    The Light Runs Deep 40

Turning Towards the Dark

    Illumine the Spirits.. 43

    Lost Woman Who Was Found...................... 44

    Exiled to the Streets.......................................46

Contemplations 48

Dark Odyssey 50

Angel of Sadness 51

Unveiling 52

Haunting Questions 53

Waiting and Wanting 55

The Mother Portal

Mothers of the World 59

Ghost Mother 61

Hot Coals 64

Phoenix 66

The Hand of Death

Ending 71

Death Wears Violets 74

Portal to Silence 75

After You've Gone 76

A Way of Dying 77

"People Will Wonder Why I'm Crying" 79

Bowing to Silence and Light

The Way 83

The Light Will Show Us 84

Oh... 85

Prayer 86

Be Ready 87

In These Turbulent Times 89

Poem 90

Called to the Ocean 91
The Light of Defeat 92

The Here and Now

Gesture 95
Trust Fall 96
Only Sky 97
Just This 98
Can I Speak Your Name? 99
Wings 101
Heartbeat 102
Quiet 103

About the Author 105

Ordinary Grace

FACES

Every face
the Divine.

Every day
one hundred times
we miss our chance.

Eyes cast downward,
we shuffle along the sidewalk
as if we are alone,
alone on this crowded street
of Angels.

TELL THE STORIES

Take dictation
from the flat stones
in the river bed.
They hold secrets.

Attend a gathering of trees.
Watch them celebrate
in the wind.

Fall into
Earth's belly.
Hear Her cries.

Find the children
who brought pieces
of heaven with them.
Ask them what life looks like.

Make your way through the dark nooks
bends
hideouts
of the city.

Touch hearts
with our forgotten sisters and brothers.
Invite them to speak their naked hurt.

Converse with
illness
healing
birth
death
and
the Infinite.

Sink into long, quiet times.
Turn towards the fissures and stars
in your heart.
Study your heart
from the inside.

Now tell the stories.

EVERY LIFE

Every life
wants to bloom
Sacred.

HOW WE ARE HELPED

I cut out tiny shapes
from Japanese papers:
fans
cranes
temples
butterflies
chrysanthemums,
glue them
in harmonious relationships
to the paper
to each other
to my eyes, hand and heart.

I draw anything and everything:
small, detailed
fish
stones
leaves
landscapes
houses
doors
gates
shoes
umbrellas
in pen and ink,
then brighten them

with color.

A memory.
Young me
settled in a corner of my room
cutting out paper dresses
for paper dolls,
stringing together tiny glass beads,
painting miniature ceramic pieces:
tea cups
hearts
horses
angels.
Feeling safe
with glimmers of joy.

Being found me,
gave me ways
to stay steady
in this uncertain world
and helped me
trust beauty
as a compass.

NOURISHING THE POET

Children speak poetry
when we sprinkle
every serving
of oatmeal
with bits
of enchanted Light
from our souls.

MYSTIC JAMMIES

I wear silk jammies
that feel like my granddaughter's
soft, buttery cheek
under my fingers
when I gently awaken her.

When the world is harsh or
her mommy's tired voice
sounds far away,
perhaps she'll find a Grandma
skin-heart memory
to soothe her.

Bent over her crib,
I soften my gaze
so she will build trust.

I pluck away fear
and other jangled thoughts
so that when she falls into my eyes
she finds shimmery meadows
that open into vast, clear space.

I brush away a deep, old tear of regret
that I could not give this to her mother.

BUTTERFLY MEDICINE

This is the grandchild
who is sick
and this is the grandmother
who is afraid
for this child.

This child
is as kind
and gentle
as the butterfly
that lands
on her shoulder,
then spends the afternoon
with us.

This child
wants to take care
of animals,
is sad because
"We can't have pets,"
is happy because
"Daddy might get me a fish."

This child
invites the butterfly,
whom she names "Golden,"

onto her finger.

This child is as gentle
with "Golden"
as this butterfly
is with the world.

SARAH KISSES

Sarah kisses often,
and always
as if it's a butterfly wing
she cherishes
and must touch.

At the age of four
she still kisses
chairs
tables
the air
the plate of rice, beans and salsa
lady bugs
tree trunks
leaves
my hand
her mama everywhere
books
and her blankie.

Yesterday,
she gently bunched up
the loose skin
on my elbow
and her eyes seemed to say,
"I understand, Grandma."

Then she kissed
my elbow
as if it was a butterfly wing.

THE SHAPE OF COMFORT

Cat
on her window throne
softening her bones
into the shape of comfort.

Passersby notice her serenity,
pause,
question
their own lives,
then quickly
move on.

THIS BED WILL NEVER END

We were made of promises,
then phone calls
with questions
in the middle,
at the end.
Sometimes "Hello" was a question.
Gestures became questions.

The bed was firm,
held us
like we wished our mothers could.

"Our bed will never end," he said.

Now
my spring sheets
are white and soft,
my bed, a blank canvas
bare
quiet
comfortable.

My bed will never end.

FADING LIGHT

I leapt
into the warm spots
you offered,
though all
on your terms.

I gave you
my light,
and I grew
dimmer,
dimmer.

HOW TO FIND POEMS

Consider everything a vast invitation.
Open wide to the unseen.
Look with mountain eyes.
Cease worshipping ordinary time.

Relax your grip.
Forget about safe routes.
Crawl into dark holes and wet tunnels.
Let yourself be scared.
Get lost.
Be found.

Let your lineage of ache teach you
and find its way to the page.
Let your lineage of wisdom teach you
and find its way to the page.

Don't believe the urgency.
Walk. Pause often. See with your feet.
Celebrate what is thriving on this planet.
Praise.
Praise often.

Listen to the pen.
Forget who you thought it belonged to.
Fall off the page.

Place yourself on the precipice of humanity.
Write what you wish you hadn't seen.

Let storms reconfigure you.
Write the before and after.

Risk expressing what's hidden
inside the folds of your life.
Invite words to bleed
and breathe onto the page.

What Illness Reveals

BEING WILL HAVE ITS WAY

"The tumor's malignant, Mom,"
my daughter tells me.

I am thrust awake.
A shattering
of my old world.

A knowing.
This is the next fire.

A knowing.
This changes everything   again.

A knowing.
You will be a howling tantrum.
You will be dignity itself.
You will let the kids rub your bald head.
You will bejewel yourself with scarves.
You will be tired.
You will be sick.
You will feel helpless,
and
you will surrender.

A knowing.
The soft light that glows through you,

no matter what,
will uplift us all.

A knowing.
Being will have its way.

THE LAST CHEMO

My daughter
cries in my arms.
I silently insist
to the Universe,
"This is it. She is done. You can't have her again."
Then, I whisper in her ear,
"It's over."

When I first got the call,
sensing what was coming,
my mother prayer:
"If this has to be,
let her lie back
on a soft pillow,
let life glide her along.
Let loving human hands
and Angels
guide her journey.
Let me remember
she belongs to the Universe.
She is life's child,
not mine."

Your devoted friends
take the perfect selfies.
Hugs,

offerings,
tips for growing your hair back.
They seem to be with you
all the time.

Balloons
with pink ribbons,
smiley faces,
butterflies.
Nurses humming Pomp and Circumstance.
A chemo achievement certificate.
Poignantly absurd.

I remember
when I wasn't there,
and wonder,
"What part did that play
in this illness?"
What was it like ages one, two, three,
to run into tentative arms,
to have a young, frightened mother,
too damaged to hold herself
let alone another?
"How scarred were you?
How deeply lonely?"

Yes, I have become the mother
I could not be.
And that is good.

But, sometimes these questions burn
in my heart...

YOU ARE BROKEN
AND YOU ARE WHOLE

This morning,
you are shining blonde hair,
full belly laughing,
a field of glow.
My heart falls into place.

I remember you
clutching your belly
on the cold tile floor
in the Boston hotel,
writhing
burning
silent screams.
You needed me
to stay back.
I have never felt so helpless.

Disease is a cauldron,
boils us to the core,
disrupts
dismantles
strips layers of seeming safety.
Disease keeps us in not knowing,
stretches us beyond
where we think we can go.

Forges us in its heat.
Transforms.
Humbles.

You tend to this wisely
in your quiet ways.
Grace is known to you.
Pain and fire,
the teachers that
turn you towards
the Sacred.

I do not know
all the ways of your mind
or see all the times
you fall to your knees.
Yet it is clear today
by your restful smile
that you are watering
holy seeds
and sit, cupped,
in the hands of the Universe.

THE LIGHT RUNS DEEP

She can barely speak.
Bee hive of doctors.
Sharp lights.
Piercing beeps.
"What state do you live in?
Who is the president?"

Mom clutches my hand.
Her fear ice cold in my veins.
I try to soften,
remember the Light that we are,
see beyond this prison,
speak that to her with my eyes.
That's all we have now—
and touch.

Let her transfusion be blood and Light,
Let the liquid be Divine nectar.
Let Love speak through me.
May she fully receive it.

Let us breathe deeply,
surrender,
move with life on its terms.

Turning Towards the Dark

ILLUMINE THE SPIRITS

Trust
that you were
not an accident,

that you hadn't
quite believed
your Light,

that you needed
to come into
this dark time,

that you needed
to heal
the remnants
of your doubt.

Then, brush
the dirt
off the lantern
you have always been
and illumine
the spirits
waiting
in the dark.

LOST WOMAN WHO WAS FOUND

You are missing sentences
teeth
fresh vegetables
a pillow.
You are missing
warm bread
and hope.

Your stomped-on heart
on your sleeve
and in the cracks around your eyes.
Broken gait.
Arms that gave up
reaching to nowhere.

Your stomped-on heart
bleeds lonely
bleeds loud
bleeds onto the sidewalk.

Buddha's having a busy day,
then sees you
when he turns the corner.
"Hello," he says,
 relaxed and kind.
"Someone has left you behind."

A tear in his eye.
He offers a hand,
relaxed and kind.

You become his day.
He decides to stay
forever
if need be,

if need be.

EXILED TO THE STREETS

Your eyes burn.
The cold wind,
not your friend today,
whips you
as we do
with our silence.

Your eyes burn
holes in me
that I quickly fill
with my to-do list.

One gaze
between us
haunted me last night.
Restless, hot, sweaty,
I wanted you gone.

But you were a force,
persistent and large,
a presence
at the foot of my bed,
unwavering.
With the sovereignty
of a redwood, you said,
"We share the same heart.

Only, my scars can be seen."

CONTEMPLATIONS

In these troubled times,
are we closer to the roots
as we witness a shattering of the old
as vaults of dark secrets
are being cracked open?

Are we relieved
that scabs are being
ripped off
and wounds can be seen
and breathe at last?

Do we feel our buried grief
and the unspoken laments
of our ancestors
as we let in the heartbreak
of our abandoned sisters and brothers
who've been cast out for centuries?

Is the inhumanity
firing us up
to love more?

Can we show our tails now?
Come out of hiding?
Get real?

Be whole?

And what about the Earth?
Can we see what we have destroyed
and cry for Her?
Help Her?

Are we able
to see our Oneness
and commit to foster healing?

Are we now inspired
to gather in the streets,
at altars,
in temples,
at the sea,
and become humble
before the Divine?

DARK ODYSSEY

When you cannot see stars,
dive headlong
into the dark.

The ancients,
who know
what binds you and what will help,
will welcome you.

They will hold you
until you feel safe
and the sobs
trapped from lifetimes
burst free.

They will whisper wisdom
and reveal
the ways and gifts
of darkness.
You may be reshaped.

You may remember
the Light of this world
and feel the stars
in your heart
that have always been.

ANGEL OF SADNESS

She extends her hand.
Stone, I am.
Stone.

Sadness says,
"You will fall.
I will be with you.
You will break.
I will take the pieces
and turn them into gold.
You will wail an ocean.
I will teach you to swim.
You won't know who you are.
I will walk beside you
as you shed the skins
you never were."

UNVEILING

In the Sacred
Silence of Being,
our heart scars
are illumined—
an invocation.

They have
been waiting for
our welcome.

HAUNTING QUESTIONS

Your life.
Your death,
by your own hand.

Were you a gossamer-winged child
who felt the world
too hard,
too cold?
Were there holes in you
where Mother Love
should have been?

Were you clay
others tried to mold,
a paint-by-numbers painting–
when you ached for
raw, primal strokes
of love
and true feeling?

Did you seek across continents,
unable to find
a sweet spot for yourself?

Did you long for a land
where motherless children

are scooped up
at the faintest scent of fear,
where lies are left at the door
and the wounded are cradled
in circles of care?

My mind seeks
a place to put you,
a safe port,
so the gnawing will stop.
Life will not give me that.

So now I sit—
at times in deep peace,
everything in its right place.
At other times—
an agitation.

I sit
with this fierce gift from you–
the Mystery.

WAITING AND WANTING

You sit
pen in hand
waiting
and wanting
to write,
like
waiting
and wanting
to cry.
The sobs are there,
below.

There is
a frozen place
that does not like
your insistence,
wants you to
be still
and
tend lovingly
to the fear
of melting.

The Mother Portal

MOTHERS OF THE WORLD

Dear Mothers of the World,
You with children
whose bodies are torn or broken,
or whose tortured feelings rip
like shards of glass
across your heart.

Millions of us in a circle
of sadness and tender love.
Our arms braided together.
We are soothing,
being soothed,
reassuring,
holding on,
holding up.

When unnecessary words
fall away,
and silence envelops us,
there is one low moan
that thunders
from the belly
of Mother Earth and
one piercing scream
that reaches back in time.

This mother burn is holy.
It has taken us beyond ourselves.
We can embrace any child
with any wound now.
We have unearthed
the treasures of
fierce devotion
and unselfish hearts.

This mother burn,
this purifying fire,
this initiation
into the ways
of the compassionate warrior
is our blessed path.

GHOST MOTHER

My empty Mom
held me
but could not feel
the invitation
of my skin,
could not feel
souls mingling,
could not receive the
sweetness
goodness
warmth
my tiny body offered,
could not smile
at the new world
I saw
with my new eyes.

Lonely.
Both of us.
Lonely.

Mom, my dear Mom,
innocent,
simply repeating
the 'ghost mother' bloodline.

Innocent.
All innocent.

Armored strangers for years,
then your falls
the emergency rooms
hospital beds
the beginning
of the steep decline.
Illness and pain
delivered us
to each other.

I cracked in the hospital
outside your door
hearing you plead and cry
to the nurses
to let you go home.
"I want to go home!" you wailed.

I found you
through the ache in your heart
that exploded when life
hit too hard.
You found me, Mom,
in the softness and care
that could come forward now.

I stopped needing you

to be Saint Mother,
accepted life's plan.

We did it, Mom.
We made it,
and untied a stubborn knot
in the bloodline.

HOT COALS

Every time I open
her front door,
I listen
towards her room
with hope
and fear.
Moans?
Groans?
Whimpers?
Silence?
I so want to remember
the Divine.

I take a step.

Is a nest of death being prepared?
Is this form
of the Great Mother,
my mother,
leaving?

Hot coals.
No choice
but to walk them.
I'm sure I can't.
Wisdom whispers,

"You are being held."
My strategies dissolve.
Blessings arrive
just when it seems impossible.

There is only Now,
and it is okay.

I move forward.

We are both in the Mystery.
We are both on hot coals.
This I know.

PHOENIX

Dusk.
The day and I
quiet
as snow.

Underbelly
of the morning
surfaces
in this welcoming stillness.

My daughter's Facebook post.
A few words and emojis
about pain
and prayers.

Moms know
when the ache
is deep.

I don't want to feel
this body
this chill of fear
this howl
that echoes back
25 years.
I don't want to remember.

I don't want to feel.

My daughter, though,
is a phoenix,
rebirth from ash
again
and
again.
These holy memories of her
coming back strong
are here, too.

Dusk.
The day and I
quiet
as snow.

The Hand of Death

ENDING

Your body
folding in
on itself.

You are, they say,
nearing the end.

Your words
farther apart.

Fewer and fewer forays
down the hall.
The walker you despise.
"That's for old people," you say, at eighty-eight.
Your small world.
The bathroom, the kitchen, the front hall table,
where you gather your precious coupons.

Pill bottles
carefully arranged,
the way you tried
with your life.
The Temazepam
that the doctor finally conceded to
after you wore him down,
that you count and count

and guard with your fear.

Blaring TV.
Law and Order, Criminal Minds, British mysteries.
A world to figure out.
The Honeymooners, I Love Lucy, Seinfeld.
A world to make you laugh.
Rachel Maddow, Anderson Cooper,
Andrea Mitchell.
A world to worry about.

Altar items on the bed.
Pictures of us.
A 45-year-old love note from Dad.
A 3 x 5 card–
"Do what you fear. Watch it disappear."
A large magnifying glass for TV weekly.
Candy for your unhappiness.
A glass bell to signal need.

At times you are content
in the cocoon
awaiting your flight.
At times you curl,
helpless,
bereft,
afraid,
while the pain sears everything.

At times you love our love.
At times you hate us all.

The true task
for me is
to love you and accept what is,
to remember the Divine messengers,
let them touch
and speak to you
through me,
when you feel
abandoned by God.

You are,
they say,
nearing the end.
We feel it.

I can also sense a beginning.
Can you?

DEATH WEARS VIOLETS

Death welcomed her.
She did not have to struggle.
Perfume in the air.
A quiet I had never felt before.
A full and holy absence.
She eased away.

If it was just Mom and me,
I might have crawled
under the covers,
curled
beside the shell of her body,
lay my head on her chest
and sobbed
a thunderous downpour.
I might have thrown my arms to the sky
with profound gratitude
for the gentleness that welcomed her
at the end.

Instead, I sat beside her,
held her hand
and cried quietly.
Mom would have loved my composure.

PORTAL TO SILENCE

Kissing her forehead
for the last time.
Feeling her meet Light.
We merge in Silence.

AFTER YOU'VE GONE

Raindrops of grief
on a bright sunny day.

A WAY OF DYING

I watched you die, Jackson
the falling away
of
hair
voice
control,
witnessing every part and function
of your body
slip away,
and your thriving gift store,
South of Market happening place,
passing on
to other hands.
You
watching
crying
watching
crying.
Then, always,
letting go.

The cavernous wound in your neck
oozing infection   and you
learning to swallow
in a different way.
Your movements slower,

more deliberate,
in response to the pain
and the wasting away   and you
learning to live
in a different way,
a way of dying,
a sacred way of dying.

Your dying taught me about living.
The ease in my joints
clarity of vision
fluidity of speech
are gifts to savor   and
they are on loan.

You died in dignity
with
gaping sores
hairless
skin and bones
dark circles
speechless
fingers with only microscopic gestures.

You emanated a light
that brought me
to my knees
in the presence
of such Grace.

"PEOPLE WILL WONDER WHY I'M CRYING"

"People will wonder why I'm crying,"
my husband says to me.
After walking through the house quietly,
he sits on the side of our bed
and cries softly.
He's not the shaking tempest I can be,
leaping from room to room,
damaging toes along the way.

He cries quietly
walks softly
transports spiders outside
with kindness and ease.

There aren't emergencies in his world.

My husband
loses his mother
and finds his deep heart.

I watch him mourn.
It is simple.
She is gone.
A great love.
Many tears.

A cave.

Long sighs.

He emerges.

Motherless.

Connected.

Strong.

"I survived what I have feared forever."

I read him this poem.

He cries quietly.

Bowing to Silence and Light

THE WAY

Beacons of Silence
are lighting
my way.

THE LIGHT WILL SHOW US

In spite of us,
Light will continue
to bless
and shine
into every opening,
and onto asphalt,
metal,
and steel.

Light will blanket
tight fists,
stiff bodies,
all the jagged edges.

Light will show us
who we are.

May we remember
and remember
and remember
This.

OH

Moon
silver sliver
in the silent sky
captures my eye
and soul.

Oh,
luminous face of God.

PRAYER

May we share
every wisp of Grace
that finds us.

BE READY

I

Be ready
when a dot
of Light
pierces
your curtain of tears,

when a duck
wants your attention,
has something important to say,

when a monk
walks by
 and whispers,
"Happiness arrives
when you welcome
Silence."

II

Be ready
to leave
it all
if the compass
spins and spins,

to glimpse
a string of stars
in the midst
of a bad dream,

to see
your ancestors
free,
guided by your mom
who found Light
in her precious
last hours.

IN THESE TURBULENT TIMES

When I remember
to listen

beneath the crashing waves
I hear the peace

and deep pulsing heart
of Mother Ocean

praying for us all.

POEM

I am listening
for the language of Light.

I am listening
for bare, transparent words
to illuminate the page.

Black ink.
White paper.
Foray into the Silence.

I am listening,
a bird
listening to the sky.

CALLED TO THE OCEAN

Frenzied.
Worried.
Anxious.
A thick carpet
of bees
swarming in my head.

A big wave
sweeps away
the carefully crafted
sand castle.
The children roar
with laughter.

My mind becomes
the ocean.

THE LIGHT OF DEFEAT

Holding my bony mother
beside her photos
of my round grandbabies.

Sense gives way.

I wanted only springtime.

Now the seasons converge.

Deep bow
to That
which allows me
to admit defeat.

The Here and Now

GESTURE

You can stop hurting yourself
with your wanting
with a kind and simple gesture
of falling into Here.

TRUST FALL

I trust You now
when You tell me
to feel
the Grace
of loss
and I see
the glow
in every stone,
the radiance behind
every
sad face.

You tell me
to just keep
turning over
my life
and
softening
into Love.

ONLY SKY

The mind
keeps breaking open
until I am only sky.

You keep asking
for coherent strands
of words
about times
before Now.

To appease you,
to be loved,
I craft
a story.

Now I feel like crying.
The sky so far away.

JUST THIS

A tree falls on my roof.
You can't reason with a storm.
This was not punishment.

Just This.

CAN I SPEAK YOUR NAME?

Can I speak your name
and feel the nameless?

Can I sob from the toes up
beside my daughter
burning in pain
her pain / my pain
every mother's pain
every being's pain
held in the painless
until
until?

Can I know this hand
this pen
moving in a rhythm
that feels close to the heartbeat
and
know nothing at all?

Can I tend to the me
who cries her tears
and their tears
bandages the teddy bears'
broken hearts
and her own

and know
there is nothing to heal
and no one healing?

Can the seeking stop here?

Koans
that are feared and cherished,
that make no sense to the mind,
yet offer the deepest peace.

WINGS

Let Grace uproot us,
drop us into koans.
Let the mind
have wings
until we know
in our bones
we are not tethered,
there was never a prison,
we do not need directions,
we do not need to know,
nothing can be held,
the sky cannot be measured.

HEARTBEAT

The seeker
removes her worn shoes,
embraces the Stillness,
gives in
to the heartbeat.

QUIET

When I am quiet
as frogs
who stop croaking
when we trespass
their sacred marsh,

when I am quiet
as a child
who is sad
in every cell,

when I am quiet
as the moment
death
carried Mom away,

I become the Here of my life,
time just another thought.

About the Author

Susanne West is a writer, poet, professor of psychology and spiritual mentor. She was on the faculty of John F. Kennedy University for thirty years and taught classes in the Consciousness and Transformative Studies and BA Psychology Programs. Susanne received the Harry L. Morrison Distinguished Teaching Award at JFKU. She also served as Chair of the Department of Liberal Arts and Director of the BA Psychology Program.

Susanne has worked in community organizations and private settings with individuals and groups since 1984, specializing in psychospiritual growth and transformation, writing and creative expression. She is the founder of two writing programs – Words with Wings and Deep Writing.

She is the author of *Soul Care for Caregivers: How to Help Yourself While Helping Others*. *Subterranean Light* is her first poetry collection.

www.susannewest.com

Also Published by Enlightened Hyena Press

Authentic Happiness in Seven Emails
by Javy W. Galindo

Sleep Paralysis
by Ryan Hurd

By His Touch
by Rolando Y. Dy Buco

www.ingramcontent.com/pod-product-compliance
Lightning Source LLC
Chambersburg PA
CBHW071721040426
42446CB00011B/2166